SEEKING A
Simpler Spirit

❋

Journal

A Reader's Digest Simpler Life ™ Book
Conceived and written by Deborah DeFord

Reader's Digest General Books

Editorial Director **Fred DuBose**
Senior Designer **Susan Welt**
Project Designer **Barbara Lapic**
Editorial Manager **Christine R. Guido**

Editor-in-Chief **Christopher Cavanaugh**
Art Director **Joan Mazzeo**

Contributors

Illustrations **Charlene Rendeiro**

Text copyright © 1999 Deborah DeFord
Copyright © 1999 The Reader's Digest Association, Inc.

Library of Congress Cataloging-in-Publication Data

DeFord, Deborah H.
    Seeking a simpler spirit journal / Deborah DeFord.
      p.   cm.
    ISBN 0-7621-0129-6
    1. Devotional calendars. 2. Spiritual journals. I. DeFord,
  Deborah H. Seeking a simpler spirit. II. Title.
  BV4811.D37 1999
  291.4'4—dc21   98-50305

SEEKING A
Simpler Spirit

Journal

with reflections by
DEBORAH DeFORD

Reader's Digest

The Reader's Digest Association, Inc.
Pleasantville, NY/Montreal

With every turning of
the page, with every bend in the
road, may you encounter God.

The newest member of our family watches my mouth intensely, as though nothing else exists as I speak to him and smile. Already his relentless observation has taught him to smile in return. Sounds and syllables will follow soon. I'm humbled to consider how my soul's expressions would develop if I gave such concentrated attention to God.

We usually use the word "cocoon" to refer to safety and coziness. Yet for the creature in nature, leaving that safe, insulated place is the only path to growth and renewal. What we cherish most because of its familiarity and comfort may be the very thing that stunts our soul.

Stretching exercises. We begin with short, stiff muscles. It hurts to bend. Our toes are impossibly distant from our finger-tips. We cannot force the muscles to lengthen quickly. But with patience and perseverance, we coax them by tiny degrees. Each inch of progress increases the flow of fresh blood and builds our vitality. So too our reach for God.

I counted twenty-eight varieties of peppers in the local farm market. I feel certain that other varieties must exist in other places around this country, not to mention the world. Some have been developed by breeding, but many occur in nature. Imagine. God gave that much creative attention to a single member of the vegetable world.

My father owned and operated a business that produced scent conditioners, the products used to fill a room with a pleasant smell. He chose essential oils from nature for all his scents, and everything that left his plant carried an unmistakable olfactory trace of its origins. It smelled great. Am I often enough in the presence of God to carry a spiritual trace of my divine connection?

The Psalmist wrote that the "heavens declare the glory of God." Since then, we have used the creative, inventive natures inherited from our creator to build ever more powerful tools to observe those heavens. We discover that we are still only scratching the surface of what the heavens contain. God's glory indeed. The Psalmist didn't know the half of it.

God is spirit, yet Michelangelo depicted the touch of God's "hand" in creation and made us sense God's presence in a powerful picture. I've watched a carpenter at work on a fine piece of cabinetry. He wields one tool, then runs his hand over the surface of his work. Another tool is needed, and this too he applies to his creation. He'll repeat this painstaking process again and again. As many times as the work requires. As many tools as it takes.

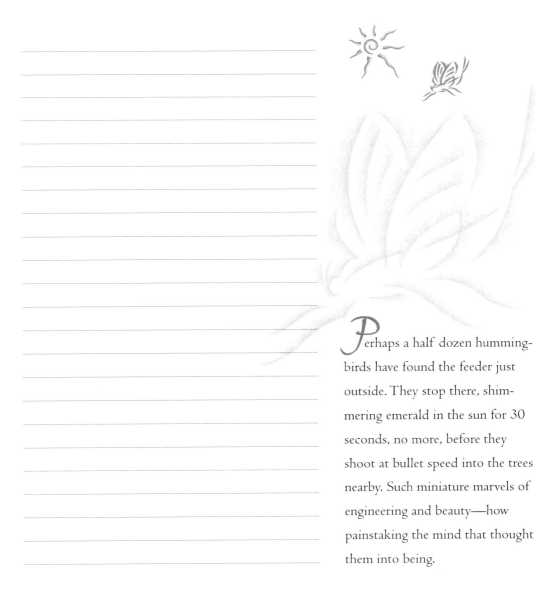

Perhaps a half dozen humming-birds have found the feeder just outside. They stop there, shimmering emerald in the sun for 30 seconds, no more, before they shoot at bullet speed into the trees nearby. Such miniature marvels of engineering and beauty—how painstaking the mind that thought them into being.

*I*f I could fit God within the bounds of human understanding, I would in terror acknowledge that humankind created its God, and not the reverse. I am content to accept moments of clarity about the nature and quality of God as the transcendent gifts they are. I am relieved to let the limitless reality of God remain mysterious.

Last year, horticulturists predicted the loss of vast numbers of dogwood trees due to disease. This year, weather conditions have given us the most spectacular dogwood season in years. Just suppose we had destroyed the trees to control the disease. God reminds us once again to be prepared for surprises in a universe we don't control.

This fragile vessel we call our body offers daily reminders that it won't last forever. It reminds us to turn anew to what lasts forever, to give more of our energy to the care and feeding, exercise and grooming of our soul.

Every so often a season of sun storms, bursts of power that radiate from our life-giving star, disrupt satellite transmissions and all that depends on them. We shudder to think of having our human-made systems "down," and we call it a disaster. We forget to be thankful that God's solar system is still "up" and running.

I'm going to conquer this,"
I tell the golf pro on the driving
range, my teeth clenched. "I'm
going to make this swing perfect."
I expect him to be gratified, even
proud, at my determination,
but he shakes his head instead.
"Golf is not a game of perfect,"
he tells me. "You just keep
getting closer and enjoy the ride."
Golf lessons for life—God
doesn't demand perfect, but offers
a course set in that direction,
expects us to practice, and invites
us to delight in it.

A group of us in the
science editor's office huddled
around a cassette tape player.
"This is the male of the pod," the
editor explained. "He's singing
to the others." An impossibly
deep, mournful vibration swelled
then diminished, again and again.
"Now listen," said the editor, a
delighted smile on his face.
Lively, trilling, familiar birdsong
filled the room—or so we thought.
"That's the same recording," he
said, "played at a fast speed."
Whalesong and birdsong.
One Composer.

I thought I was the only one who remembered after more than 35 years. But on a recent visit, my sister unearthed the same memory. An extended family Christmas, fire crackling in the fireplace, the tree's blue lights reflecting on the gold ornaments. Young and old together and wrapped in rare, still harmony, listening to Tchaikovsky's violin concerto. This, God's Christmas present of a family together, we remember above all the others.

One variety of tree shoots its main trunk straight skyward. Another meanders with gentle turns and graceful switches. Then there is the evergreen that seems to crouch in self-defense against the elements or with some special love of the earth beneath it. One is not better or more beautiful than the other. How like the course of human lives. God knows how each of us will grow and wants to make us a work of unique beauty.

I spotted a young child wandering alone down the hall in the public library. Twenty paces behind and keeping out of sight was Mom, following and watching. The child reached the big doors that led outside and stopped. Panic struck. His face crumpled. Lesson learned, Mom relented and hurried into view to hold and comfort him. We, too, can feel we've wandered out of God's view and care. We learn the truth when we turn and admit we're lost.

The full moon's ability to catch some of our Sun's brilliance and offer it to us anew turned the ocean into a field of sparkling diamonds last night. We could hope to become moons to God's Sun, and help illuminate the lives around us.

*E*very growth in our
character that God enacts
requires a sacrifice in us. We gain
the courage to cooperate with
God by focusing not on what we
give up—our weaknesses and
limitations and hurtful habits—
but on what giving them up
gives in return. We want to hang
on to our crutches. God wants
us to fly.

Outside my window, the
eggs have hatched at last. This
morning, I heard the chirping
and saw the big tulip mouths
agape on matchstick necks, vying
for earthworm bits brought by
the mother bird. Such tiny
creatures given such miraculous
provision.

I'm never more present than when I'm cooking!" one person declares. "For me," says another, "it's in a canoe on white water." Still another chimes in, "In the darkroom, developing my photographs." These are the moments God gives us to live, to make the most of, to appreciate.

I always know when I've planted a flower in the wrong place. It cranes its neck, growing overlong to find the light it requires. Or it droops and drops its leaves because of a lack of ground moisture. Or it simply withers away beneath surrounding plants that are better placed. God has suited us for a particular soil— it's a sign worth noticing when our neck grows stiff, our spirit dulls, or our energy fails.

Scripture acts as an owner's manual for human life. We try and fail at loving God with our whole selves. We try and fail at loving others as we love ourselves. We even try and fail at loving ourselves. Now, we can just keep trying in the hope that we will finally somehow figure out what's going wrong. Or we can consult the Maker in Scripture and get the Expert's word on the subject.

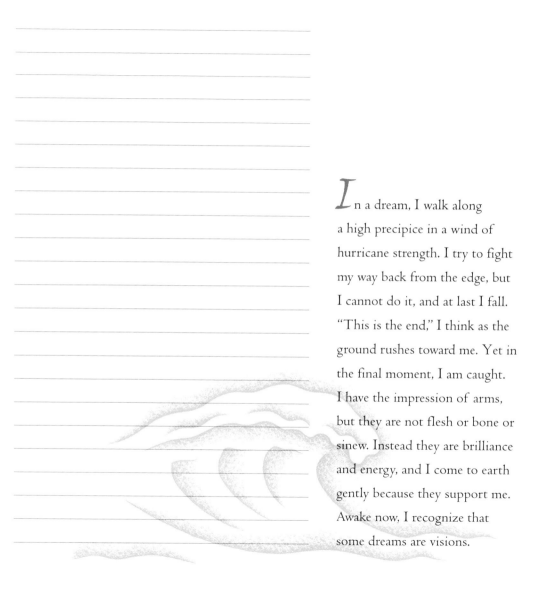

*I*n a dream, I walk along
a high precipice in a wind of
hurricane strength. I try to fight
my way back from the edge, but
I cannot do it, and at last I fall.
"This is the end," I think as the
ground rushes toward me. Yet in
the final moment, I am caught.
I have the impression of arms,
but they are not flesh or bone or
sinew. Instead they are brilliance
and energy, and I come to earth
gently because they support me.
Awake now, I recognize that
some dreams are visions.

I watched a weaver working on a hand loom. I saw her past work, resplendent in dense colors and textures. She showed me the pattern she had designed for the work in progress. But her work at the loom itself could only be accomplished one strand of yarn at a time, one inch of fabric at time. We want the picture whole, right now, but God is weaving a work of true beauty that must accumulate over time.

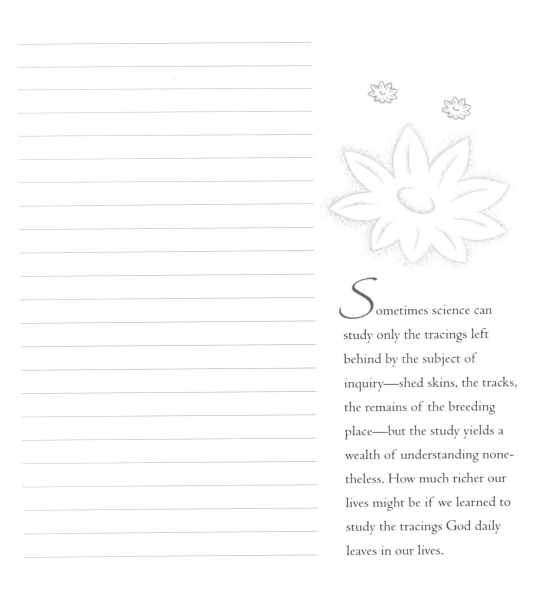

*S*ometimes science can study only the tracings left behind by the subject of inquiry—shed skins, the tracks, the remains of the breeding place—but the study yields a wealth of understanding nonetheless. How much richer our lives might be if we learned to study the tracings God daily leaves in our lives.

We follow the musings of a close friend—thoughts expressed freely, in the safety of love, and without the straight logic of a formal conversation. And we revel in the leaps and unexpected turns, because we travel through it side by side. This is the sweetness of two souls in a single framework, and it is a human taste of the divine connection.

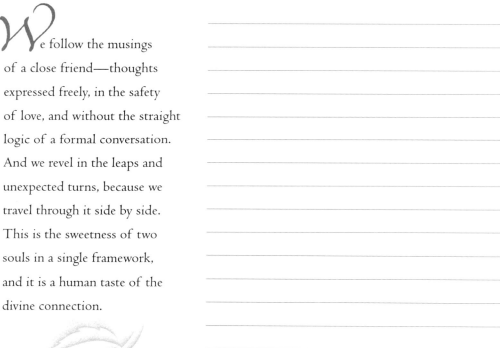

Even in the heart of a city,
trees and grasses push up through
the merest cracks and crevices of
our human construction. In this
way, God reminds us who gave
us the gift of creativity.

We await the verdict, the diagnosis of a tiny dark lump found growing where it doesn't belong, and think dark thoughts of mortality and the loss of someone we love so dearly. We forget that we are all under sentence of death. Why don't we live every day knowing this is the only day we have?

When the old barn finally fell to pieces for want of upkeep, the locals came to redeem its parts. One man gathered the boards that had long been home to wood-eating insects. He might have filled the holes and painted the wood and made it look no different from some new, quickly processed lumber. He rubbed it smooth and oiled it instead, letting the wood's original grain and the life it had sustained become its unique beauty. Just so, let God redeem us with all the marks of life still on us.

One mechanical failure follows another, from transmission to furnace to the plumbing under the toilet— things falling apart as temporary things always will. I turn my attention once again to the things that are forever, worthy of at least as much maintenance and a lot more reflection.

*I*f I hadn't seen the grasshopper
arrive, his bright yellow-green
body exposed in flight, I would
never have picked him out later
on the rocky ledge, so perfectly
did his gray-speckled resting self
blend in. It is one more protective
provision from the Maker to
let life continue.

Watching a softball game from a distance, the observer sees the bat strike the ball, then waits a second and a half before the sound of impact arrives. Just because we haven't yet heard God in the present moment doesn't mean that grace isn't already in play. In both cases, the sound is inevitable. The action has already occurred.

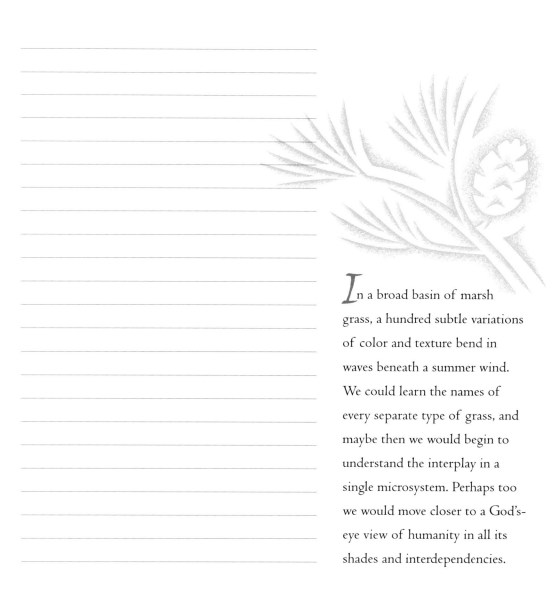

*I*n a broad basin of marsh grass, a hundred subtle variations of color and texture bend in waves beneath a summer wind. We could learn the names of every separate type of grass, and maybe then we would begin to understand the interplay in a single microsystem. Perhaps too we would move closer to a God's-eye view of humanity in all its shades and interdependencies.

*I*f we could free within us
the pioneer spirit that propelled
individuals across oceans when
people still believed the world
was flat, what wonders among
God's best intentions for us
might we discover?

How can God be equally God—present and active—to all of creation, all at once? This is a conundrum to human understanding that makes me think of an ocean, equally present at all times on all its shores, wearing and replenishing landscapes, supporting billions of acres of life in its depths, making weather, evaporating, condensing, continuing.

Regrettably, the omni-
present litigation in modern
society supports the delusion
that we can put a monetary value
on life. We can't create life, nor
can we buy it. We can only
protect and cherish it as the
gift that it is.

*T*ouch a snail and it becomes a creature tucked out of reach within its hard shell. Wait and watch silently and it will re-emerge, capable again of feeling and forward motion. Maybe God takes the silent approach with us at times to coax us out from behind our fearful defenses.

I watch a photographer changing the attachments on her camera, searching for the best way to make an authentic representation of what she has seen. One camera, one subject, but a choice of many lenses. What better to hope for in life than the lens that will give us an authentic view of what God has provided?

A piece of fruit contains the future of its kind in the least attractive of its parts, its pit. We can't know by appearance what will prove most vital. Would Jonah have guessed that a big hungry fish was his second chance with God?

A painting in a local museum depicts a crowd in a place and time when a person was not dressed without hat on head. A marvelous collection of caps and toques, bowlers and broad brims—each with details to set the wearer apart—dots the canvas. How stunning to realize that the hats don't begin to describe how uniquely God has fashioned the human hearts of their wearers.

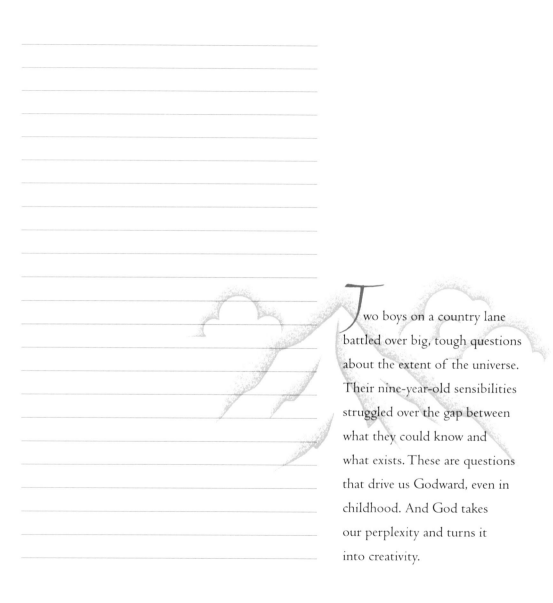

Two boys on a country lane battled over big, tough questions about the extent of the universe. Their nine-year-old sensibilities struggled over the gap between what they could know and what exists. These are questions that drive us Godward, even in childhood. And God takes our perplexity and turns it into creativity.

Some dishes—stews, soups, dinner pies—need time to let the separate foods and spices, herbs and essences merge, to make a flavor more complicated and delightful than any one ingredient alone. When we celebrate the individual, we can forget that God also created the community. When we rush our togetherness, we can forget that all good blends require time.

A large flock of sparrows performed an air show just outside, this morning, taking turns in sets of a dozen or more to land and splash in a field flooded by last night's storm. It's worth noting that they did not sit on a branch and mope because their field harvest of worms had been inundated. Instead they gloried in the gift of an unexpected bathing place of exceptional proportions.

A two-year-old child has learned just enough about the telephone to answer it when it rings. The art of conversation still eludes him, yet he insists that he should be in charge of the family phone. I can imagine God's smile every time we, like the two-year-old, master one tiny skill and think we know it all.

I marvel at the counterfeits of the garden—weeds that encroach as lookalikes on the cultured varieties. Only time and close observation allow us to distinguish between the plant that adds beauty and bears fruit, and the other that steals both. Life too offers both fruitful choices and the mimics that sap our strength without giving in return. God grant us the wisdom and patience to discern the difference.

Consider the finest wines and cheeses, leathers and objects of bronze—in the hands of the masters, these reach their prime only with age. Perhaps, keeping in mind the Master Creator, it's time to redefine the "prime" of human life.

A group of workers have been installing the poles needed to electrify the railroad line along an area of bedrock. I'm gratified and comforted that they have had to labor for months with jackhammers, hydraulic drills, and finally even dynamite to make a mere dimple in what God laid down.

The first time we hear the
recorded sound of our own voice,
we say, "That doesn't sound like
me at all!" But the friend beside
us replies, "Yes it does." How
gracious of God to give us one
another so we can learn not to
take our own experience as the
beginning and end of truth.

My uncle used to take us kids to a shale pit. We'd dig around in the friable rock and uncover tiny fossils, the ancient remains of snails and worms and waving ferns, all gone but not erased. As I consider that I too will leave something behind, I hope that it will include the impression of God.

Shadows are darkness without substance. They add contrast that heightens the brilliance of a lovely day. They provide clues to the location of the sun. They enable us to determine what direction we are headed and reveal what's approaching from around a blind corner. God offers shadows in life. We can fear them, or we can let them do their work of enhancing and informing and helping us see ahead.

We love the sparkle of a sunny autumn day, and sometimes forget that only under a gloomy sky do the leaves glow in their most vibrant colors. Perhaps in the same way, God coaxes out of us what's best and strongest not in our glittering, carefree times but rather in our seasons of adversity.

The lessons of an injured back: We think we'll gain the greatest benefit if we can snuggle ourselves against something soft and accommodating; we discover that what we need is solid support and a straight spine. The way to healing and the surcease of pain is often the way that seems the harder.

I was amazed recently to stumble across a list of 22 kinds of wind, each described with its particular characteristics, directions, locations, and implications. Until now I thought one single thing when I thought "wind." Imagine how much less than the reality must be our conception when we think "God."

A journey by air offers a vision. On an overcast day, what looks from land like a flat gray ceiling can appear from above as tumbling, flocculent hills on a sunny afternoon. Our lives, as well, may have one appearance when we "see" only from within ourselves. How different when we consider God's point of view.

Two water spiders perform their waltz on the pond's surface, supported by its skinlike tension. They skate with ease, unconcerned and almost certainly unaware of the water's depth or their inability to survive if submerged. It is a sign of God's mercy that we know as little as those spiders about the dangers that surround us. It is a sign of our maturity when we learn to be grateful for God's care in spite of our ignorance.

I love an after-dark walk in a neighborhood of undrawn drapes and windows opened wide; to see life going its way and hear the voices of love and cooperation; to understand that we all come from somewhere and are making our way to somewhere else. Most of all I love knowing that our whole journey traverses the palm of a single Almighty hand.

I've had a disappointing harvest of tomatoes, my first experience in container gardening after years of planting in a former cow pasture. I know now: the pots were too small, the soil underfed. I wonder how often we stunt our spiritual development with too contained a view of the possibilities and too little nourishment from the Source of life.

I found flowers pressed between the pages of an antique dictionary, someone's valiant effort to preserve a gift of evanescent beauty. Yet in trying to save this transitory gift, the preserver forestalled the cycle of rebirth. Some divine gifts are not meant to be grasped, but rather cherished with an open hand.

A heavy fog can transform the most familiar landscape into an alien and frightening place. Yet the place we know and love remains, even though the atmosphere has distorted our sense of it. We can be certain, too, that when the face of God is obscured by circumstance or by our inner turmoil, it is our perspective that has changed, not God.

To watch any member of the animal kingdom at ease is to rediscover a sense of play. We equate growing up with a commitment to seriousness and work. Yet only consider the fishing style of the pelican, the treetop travel of the chimpanzee, the gleeful social style of the otter; and then tell me that the One who made it all doesn't intend for us to enjoy ourselves.

The Lord is near to all
who call on him, to all who call
on him in truth.

Psalm 145:18